Around
Skegness

IN OLD PHOTOGRAPHS

Low tide in the Haven at Gibraltar Point, with the anchored pleasure boats aground on the mud; photographed by Henry Wilkinson in 1948.

Around Skegness

IN OLD PHOTOGRAPHS

Collected by WINSTON KIME

Alan Sutton Publishing Limited
Phoenix Mill · Far Thrupp · Stroud
Gloucestershire

First published 1994

Copyright © Winston Kime

British Library Cataloguing in Publication Data

A catalogue record for this book is available
from the British Library.

ISBN 0–7509–0644–8

Typeset in 9/10 Sabon.
Typesetting and origination by
Alan Sutton Publishing Limited.
Printed in Great Britain by
The Bath Press, Avon.

Contents

Salem Bridge and windmill at Wainfleet, *c.* 1910.

Introduction

Skegness in Old Photographs (1992) dealt solely with the seaside town, but in the present publication about half the pictures relate to the district, in a radius of a dozen miles or so from Skegness, taking in Alford and Spilsby. For historical background we need go back no further than a few decades into the nineteenth century, when branch lines were just reaching out from the East Lincolnshire Railway to Spilsby, Wainfleet and Skegness. Many places were still left a long way from a railway station and the carrier cart or the farmer's pony and trap provided the chief means of getting to market without using a lot of boot leather. Bicycles were still quite a new invention and no more than a fresh toy for the better off. Men and horses did the work on the farms, and carts and wagons carried the loads in villages and towns.

In the ten years between 1871 and 1881, Skegness increased its population almost fourfold, from 349 to 1,338. In contrast, most of the surrounding villages had declining populations: Friskney from 1,668 to 1,477; Burgh-le-Marsh, 1,236 to 1,136; Croft, 858 to 752; Ingoldmells, 301 to 241, with Wainfleet All Saints practically static, decreasing from 1,355 to 1,349. The reason for the reduction was the agricultural depression, brought on by foreign imports, bad winters and outbreaks of crop and cattle disease, sending many farmers bankrupt and land workers packing off to cities and countries overseas.

The fact that Wainfleet was just about holding its own might be attributed to the arrival of the railway in 1871, which made it a centre for transporting farm products to inland markets. Alford had had the railway since 1848 and in 1881 its population of 2,894 was slightly higher than ten years before. But in Spilsby, connected to the rail network in 1868, numbers had dropped from 1,623 to 1,549.

The railway extension from Wainfleet to Skegness in 1873 contributed to the big jump in the village population, but a much greater factor was the involvement of the landowning Earl of Scarbrough who, in the late 1870s began developing it as a watering place, a diversification exercise to counteract the recession in agriculture. New streets, houses and shops sprang up and by 1881 there had been a large influx of new residents from other parts of Lincolnshire and beyond, all hopeful of improving their lot in the new and growing seaside resort.

Skegness is frequently described as springing from a small fishing village, but it is hardly true. The census returns for 1871 show only one full-time fisherman and the male population was almost wholly employed in agriculture and craft trades. Many of the women engaged in domestic work accommodating the area's wealthier families who came down to the sea to bathe, following the fashion set by the nobility at the south coast resorts. The day of the tripper was not yet, but was in the very near future.

South and west of Wainfleet, the East Fen had only been drained in the early part of the nineteenth century, and northward, between the Wolds and the sea coast, was the great marshland plain, providing one of the richest pastures in all England. Sheep and cattle were brought to regular fairs and markets at Alford, Spilsby, Partney, Burgh and Wainfleet, while on the arable lands of Friskney and Wrangle, root and grain crops were cultivated on the fertile soil which not long before had been under water for a large part of the year. Fen drainage and enclosures had put the wildfowlers and decoymen out of business and only a few survived to make a living netting birds along the Wash shore.

At the dawn of the twentieth century the 1901 census showed the six most populous places in this part of south-east Lindsey as: Alford 2,478, Skegness 2,140, Spilsby 1,483, Friskney 1,302, Wainfleet All Saints 1,055 and Burgh-le-Marsh 974. Every other parish had below 700 inhabitants. Friskney, surprisingly high in the list, had the largest land area with 6,844 acres, although Wainfleet St Mary with 6,179 acres was not far behind. The three Wainfleet parishes of All Saints, St Mary and Northolme had an aggregate population of 1,902.

The fifty years that followed, making up the first half of the twentieth century, is the period covered by the majority of the photographs on these pages. In the last census before the Second World War – in 1931 – the largest centres of population were: Skegness 9,122, Alford 2,227, Friskney 1,599, Spilsby 1,372, Wainfleet All Saints 1,324, Burgh 916, Wainfleet St Mary 908 and Croft 825. After the war the holiday industry and retirement homes were to boost the coastal population north of Skegness, but in 1931 Ingoldmells was still a village with only 293 inhabitants and Chapel St Leonards' population was 549.

Population is not necessarily an indication of a town's importance, as exemplified by Spilsby, which was the accepted centre of a neighbourhood that was sometimes referred to as 'Spilsbyshire'. It had a weekly market, magistrates court and registry offices, and was represented in most of the essential trades, professions and social and religious activities. Only very slowly did its major administrative offices pass to Skegness and, even then, until local government reorganization in 1974, Spilsby Rural District Council took in 69 parishes and covered an area of about 220 square miles, stretching from Anderby in the north to Sibsey in the south.

Unlike Spilsby, Alford in the present century had an Urban District Council, but nevertheless it was the focal town for the villages outside the aegis of Spilsby, Horncastle, Louth and Skegness, and its Internal Drainage Board covered an area reaching to the boundaries of Skegness. Markets and courts added to Alford's importance and, like Spilsby, it had a grammar school and a Territorial Reserve of the Lincolnshire Regiment with its own drill hall. Formerly the terminus of a turnpike road and stagecoach service to London, via Spilsby and Boston, Alford was fortunate to find itself on the Boston to Grimsby route of the East Lincolnshire Railway when it opened in 1848. In 1864 an Act of Parliament authorized the construction of a branch railway from Alford to Mablethorpe, but the plan fell through for lack of financial backing. If it had gone ahead and Mablethorpe had obtained its rail connection almost ten years before Skegness it is interesting to speculate which of the two resorts would have developed more quickly.

The old squirearchy and landed gentry who reigned supreme in many rural parishes almost up to the Second World War have almost disappeared, together with their great residences. Many of these fine country houses have been demolished and others have become nursing homes, residential flats or have been put to other uses. Two that survive in this area have both overcome perils to keep alive. Harrington Hall, on the edge of the Tennyson Country, had the threat of demolition hanging over it as long ago as 1927, when it was saved by Major W.H. Rawnsley of Well Vale. Then, as most readers will recall, it was gutted by fire on 4 November 1991. That must have been a heart-breaking blow to its new owners, but they bravely performed a phoenix act to bring that fine, historic building back to life.

Gunby Hall is still an occupied house, although maintained by the National Trust. It could well have been a casualty of the Second World War, albeit the threat came not from enemy bombs, but from our own defenders. A year or two after the conflict began, the then owner-occupier, Field Marshal Sir Archibald Montgomery Massingberd, was taking his morning constitutional in the grounds when he spied several strangers hopping about among the lawns and shrubs, apparently taking photographs. They turned out to be surveyors with tripods and theodolites; when the retired FM asked them what they were up to, he was informed that ground clearance was about to begin for the new RAF Steeping Aerodrome and the tall trees surrounding Gunby Hall were in the flight path of the bombers and would have to come down. Not only that, but there was a strong possibility that the hall itself would have to be demolished for the same reason. To say the least, Sir Archibald was quite put out by this piece of news and, although history regards him as something less than a military genius, he was a man of action, and he also knew some very good telephone numbers. It was even said that he was on speaking terms with His Majesty. A week or two went by and it was then put about that the rumours that the hall was going to be knocked down were much exaggerated and the flight path of the Lancasters would not disturb a single sapling surrounding the ancestral home of the Montgomery Massingberds.

Winston Kime

By the Seaside

A picture postcard by Valentine, posted in 1911. The iron fountain, now in the Fairy Dell, is standing on the site of the present Embassy Theatre, while the fairground, with helter-skelter, big wheel and museum ship, is on the central beach.

A traffic roundabout at the Clock Tower was obviously not needed in 1907 when pedestrians had the carriageway almost to themselves.

South Parade in 1909. Although the buildings remain, the bare grass-and-bushes waste ground on the left has long been replaced by attractive amenities.

Marine Gardens, South Parade, in the 1920s, with the old lifeboathouse – in use until 1990 – partly visible far left. A flag was flown from the tall flagmast when the lifeboat was at sea. Lifeboat coxswain Matthew Grunnill, while making adjustments to the rigging, fell nearly 40 ft from the pole, injuring his spine and causing him great pain for the remainder of his long and active life. He died in 1939, aged 75.

Grand Parade, looking south from the Pier ramp in 1922, with Pier Terrace on the right, still all boarding houses. Between Prince Alfred Avenue and Edinburgh Avenue was a rough grass patch where charabancs and buses unloaded. There were no shops or cafés on the parade and the Marine Gardens were on the left, below the parade wall.

Lumley Pullover (Tower Esplanade) in Edwardian days, with plenty of wheeled traffic mingling with the holidaymakers in their wide brimmed bonnets and straw hats. The lower picture (1922), at the bottom end of the pullover, shows a number of pony carts plying for hire and a donkey-drawn phaeton for children. One supposes that the animal droppings were taken care of as carefully as they were in the streets.

Lumley Pullover, *c.* 1910, with donkey and pony sheds on either side, and pierrots and the fairground on the sands.

Tower Esplanade soon after completion in 1923, when it replaced the former Lumley Pullover. The roundabouts, swingboats, refreshment huts, etc, were still on the beach and, off the picture to the right, work had just started on the new boating lake.

Central beach in the 1890s, with the donkey and pony sheds on either side of Lumley Pullover and the museum ship, *Eliza*, sited near what is now the Boating Lake Buffet. The amusements and refreshment huts stood just above high tide mark a little to the left of the top picture. The lettering on the helter-skelter reads: 'The Skegness Sand Chute'.

In 1924 Tower Esplanade had only recently been constructed and the donkey shed on the north side was still in place, but the Café Dansant (later the Foreshore Centre) had been built on the site of the pony shed in 1911.

Donkeys on North Parade, *c.* 1912, when a ride cost only one old penny. The donkey nearest the camera is fitted with a wicker basket to carry two small children sitting back to back. The licence-holder has his official badge pinned on his waistcoat. Note the slot machines on the fence bordering the Park, or 'Jungle', from which a penny would extract a bar of chocolate or chewing-gum.

A horse and cart brings passengers across the creeks for a sail into the Wash in 1910.

Pleasure boats were still busy in the 1930s and the former Coverack (Cornwall) lifeboat – renamed *Grace Darling II* – loads up for another trip. The wooden platforms with iron wheels acted as bridges between the boats and dry land.

Walking the plank, or two planks in this case, to cross the water between beach and boat in the summer of 1923. Several boatmen stand by to assist the balancing act, with one helping passengers into the boat while another steadies it against the motion of the waves.

Ten years earlier on the same piece of beach. Children splash happily among the foaming wavelets as a sailing boat sets out with a full load for a sea trip, perhaps to the sealbanks.

Paddling was more popular in the 1920s than it is today. Grown-ups as well as children rolled up their trousers or tucked their frocks into their knickers to feel the salty ripples splashing round their ankles.

Paddling near high tide from the central beach in the 1930s, with the Pier stretching out to sea.

A long canvas windbreak sheltering the deck-chairs on a breezy day, *c*. 1920.

Samuel Lewis, outward bound, attracts a large Edwardian crowd to speed her on her way. Large bonnets and long skirts, and trilbies and ties contrast oddly with the scantily clad holidaymakers who nowadays follow the lifeboat down to the launching.

Lifeboat away, slipping off the carriage as the crew dip their oars into the deepening sea. *Samuel Lewis* was in service for more than a quarter of a century until 1932 and was the last of the sail-and-oar lifeboats at Skegness. In 1926 the launching horses gave way to a motor tractor. The flat sandplates, or 'clappers', attached to the two big wheels on the carriage prevented it from sinking in the sand.

The Brig "AZHA" of Arendal, Norway, wrecked off Skegness, November 11th, 1912. Crew of 8 saved by the Skegness Lifeboat "Samuel Lewis." :: Cox. Matt Grunnill.

Commemorative picture postcards of two brave rescues in heavy seas by Skegness lifeboat. In 1912 the *Samuel Lewis* (top) with her seventeen-man crew went to the aid of the Norwegian *Azha*. The King of Norway awarded medals to the coxswain and second cox. The stricken *Azha* afterwards broke in half. The *Anne Allen* lifeboat was launched when *Britannic* sent up distress signals off the Norfolk coast in 1937. Skegness lifeboat had rendered assistance to the same vessel more than twenty years earlier and she was again salvaged on the later occasion.

BARGE "BRITANNIC" OF LONDON. CREW OF 3 MEN AND A DOG SAVED BY THE SKEGNESS LIFE-BOAT. COXSWAIN GEORGE PERRIN. NOVR 17TH 1937.

North Parade, *c.* 1930, in the area now occupied by the Sun Castle and Natureland. The Figure 8 Switchback Railway, seen in the background, was dismantled in 1970.

The beach at the bottom of Winthorpe Avenue before the dunes had been replaced by concrete stepped walls. The Derbyshire Miners' Convalescent Home opened in 1928, shortly before this photograph was taken.

What's so different here? Ah, yes, the Sun Castle was not built until 1931–2 and in 1930 you could see the bowling greens and colonnade as you walked along North Parade.

The Waterway in 1933, two seasons after its completion. It stretched from opposite the present Town Hall as far as the Pier and was extended to Tower Esplanade in 1938. North Parade and the newly opened Sun Castle are top right, with tennis courts occupying the present Natureland site.

The open-air swimming pool which opened in 1928, pictured two years later. The domed bandstand overlooking both pool and piazza was scarcely used because of poor acoustics. The pool was not heated until many years after. Below is the three-tier diving stage.

North Parade funfair, *c.* 1923, with miniature railway, the chairoplane ride, the Figure 8 Switchback and other amusements.

The autumn illuminations began in the early 1930s (Skegness received its mains electricity supply in 1932) and here the 1954 lights are reflected in the boating lake. Butlin House on the far right and the Sandbeck House Hotel on the other side of the Clock Tower were demolished around the same time in 1972.

Skegness Pier, more than a third of a mile long, opened in 1881 and had altered little in this photograph in 1920. The ballustraded ramps on either side, ornamental gas lamps and Victorian Gothic tollgate remained until an entirely new entrance was constructed in 1937. It was replaced again in 1971 with the present entrance.

In 1911 the Pier was a fine place to breathe the invigorating air, either strolling or sitting in the sun as if on a sea voyage, with the waves below and on either side.

The Privateer steam paddleboat ran trips from the pierhead across the Wash to Hunstanton and other places and was the last of the pier steamers, ceasing business at Skegness in 1911. The top picture shows her near the Pier landing-stage. *The Privateer* had also taken excursions from Boston to Skegness and, below, she is paddling along the Witham in Boston. This popular little ship had a sad end, sinking in the English Channel in the First World War.

The great storm coinciding with a spring tide on the night of 11 January 1978 wrecked Skegness Pier and several other seaside piers around the English coast. Perhaps the first people to see the damage were the crew of the Skegness lifeboat, returning from a night search. Unable to land because of the scattered debris, they were forced to ride at anchor until daylight. The pierhead and shelters were left as two islands at high tide.

In October 1985 the final dismantling was being carried out on the pierhead when, on Saturday the 28th, an unattended incinerator sparked off a fire which destroyed the whole of the wooden fabric, leaving only the bare iron framework. Contractors afterwards moved in with blowtorches, working between tides, and the blackened skeleton was dismembered piece by piece.

There was no bus station in Skegness in the 1920s, but several different sites were used as termini by the operating companies. One was a piece of waste ground on Grand Parade between Prince Alfred and Edinburgh Avenues and here an East Midland coach had evidently brought in a load of day visitors in July 1929.

The Central Car Park, Grand Parade, photographed by G.H.F. Atkins in July 1931. A large proportion of the cars have canvas hoods and motorcycle combinations are much in evidence. It was still a grassed area and the temporary fencing in the foreground divides it from the fairly new Embassy Ballroom and bathing pool.

The parade penny-all-the-way buses ran from the Clock Tower to the Pleasureland amusement park at the far end of North Parade and this was the scene in the late 1920s. The bottom picture shows one of Tom Cary's Vulcan 'toastracks' and the board on top states that the 1d. fare would be refunded on any ride in Butlin's fairground. Both photographs were taken by G.H.F. Atkins in July 1929.

These two postcards are only 50 per cent 'old photographs', the other part being comic sketches superimposed on the foreground. They were two of a popular series on sale in the 1920s, drawn by F.H. Martin and published by C. & A.G. Lewis of Nottingham.

SECTION TWO
Streets and Buildings

The Royal Oak, Seathorne, pictured in the 1930s when motor traffic was just beginning to buzz along Roman Bank. The landlord in 1930 was William Brown.

The seaward end of Lumley Road in 1913, looking more like a pedestrian precinct. The tall terrace houses still had their front gardens and the building on the corner of Drummond Road (left) did not become the Marine Hotel until after the First World War, with shops added later.

A busy scene on the other side of Lumley Road, c. 1930, with Hercock's banana lorry passing Clements' Tower Theatre. Smith's Arcade is next door and then Watson's Tower Café and other fairly new buildings. The Tower Theatre operated as a cinema practically from its inception and, heavily bombed in 1941, it closed until rebuilding could begin after the war ended.

Lumley Terrace in the early 1880s, soon after completion of this row of boarding houses and residences. They retained their front lawns until about 1930 when, one by one, shops were built out to the pavement. This eastern end of Lumley Road, which is now a dual-carriageway, has the Beresford Avenue junction to the right of the photograph.

Osbert House Hotel, near the Clock Tower, *c.* 1920, later to become Butlin House, head office of the holiday camp chain. The building was demolished in 1972, to be replaced by shops and restaurants.

Crofts' Stores was established in 1882 when George J. Crofts arrived from Dorset and set up as 'draper, milliner, hosier and outfitters'. This was how the shop looked in the 1890s, when the street trees were only saplings. The building was demolished in 1985 and new premises built for Nationwide, Dixons and Baker's Oven.

Nestor Howell's books and stationery shop at No. 19 Lumley Road was also the post office in the 1880s and '90s, with Mr Howell as postmaster. The GPO moved to separate premises on Roman Bank and the bookshop, Avery's for many years, is now Murray's News.

Lumley Square in 1934, with demolition of old houses just commencing. Painted on the end wall is an advertisement for the RAOB (Buffaloes) Club which was to become the Skegness Working Men's Club in Briar Way. The gas showrooms were built on the site later that year, followed by new public lavatories.

The Sycamores, No. 42 High Street, was a relic of nineteenth-century Skegness. Little is known about its early history, but from around 1870 until the 1890s it was used as a seaside retreat by Spilsby solicitor West John Rainey. From 1920 until its demolition in the late 1970s the house was occupied by the Gibbins family.

Roman Bank, near Scarbrough Avenue junction, *c.* 1920. John Wholey's grocery and sweetshop, with off-licence, is on the left, next to Hubbard's and later Bill Neale's smithy, followed by hoardings and old cottages where Wilson's furnishing business is today. The Derbyshire Children's Seaside Home is on the right.

Roman Bank, *c.* 1930. On the left are Bradleys' double-fronted menswear shop, Green's shoe shop and the National School. A street sweeper's three-wheeled barrow stands on the opposite side and W.J. Cook's butchery, a little further along, has a canvas awning, like many of the others in this picture.

The Ship Hotel, *c.* 1910. The hotel stood just inside Winthorpe parish, but you could leave by either door and step across Burgh Road or Roman Bank and be in Skegness. This 1830s public house was demolished in 1936 and Winthorpe was incorporated in Skegness in 1924.

Ship Corner, at the junction of Roman Bank and Burgh Road, photographed by G.H.F. Atkins in June 1933, with a Barton bus setting off for Nottingham. A few months later work commenced on the construction of Castleton Boulevard, extending Burgh Road forward to the seafront and Skegness's first traffic lights were installed on the new crossroads.

The Pleasure Gardens – now Tower Gardens – came right up to Lumley Road in 1908.
Rutland Terrace can be seen in the background, to the left, and part of the Pavilion in
the centre.

The pond in Tower Gardens seemed to be an attraction to these schoolboys in 1905,
although there were no ducks about at that time.

Coronation Walk, the tree-lined pathway between Drummond Road and the Vine Hotel – outlined in the lower picture – and extending to Richmond Drive as Vine Walk. It commemorates the crowning of Edward VII in 1901 and is pictured just a few years later.

The ornate archway entrance with ticket office at the Arcadia Theatre, Drummond Road, with an advertisement for the Arcadia Revels of 1928 and the comedy duo of Flotsam and Jetsam, renowned on stage and radio. Portraits of the resident Arcadia artistes are also displayed. The theatre opened in 1911. In my photograph below, taken on 29 March 1988, demolition had just commenced. The site is now a council car park.

Drake Road, bordering Seacroft Golf Links, in the early twentieth century. It takes its name from the family who owned a large part of the Seacroft sea frontage. The Drakes lived at Shardeloes Park, Buckinghamshire, and inherited further Seacroft land from their relatives, the Tyrwhitts of Stainfield, near Bardney. Three iron posts at Gibraltar Point carry the initials TTD, marking the southern boundary of Thomas Tyrwhitt-Drake's estate.

Shardeloes in Shardeloes Road, a detached annexe to the Crown Hotel, in the 1920s. It was later joined onto the hotel which had earlier been known as the Links. Shardeloes Road, in the early twentieth century, was a rough surfaced private road and, to meet legal requirements, was closed to traffic one day a year by a single-bar gate, partly visible at the foot of this picture.

Sea View Road in the 1920s and, on the left, the cow pasture belonging to the white-walled farmhouse on Roman Bank, just visible in the left background. Originally a narrow track from Roman Bank to the seashore, it was known as Sea View Lane for some years after it became a proper road.

The burnt-out shell of the Council Offices, on the corner of Roman Bank and Algitha Road, after destruction by fire on the night of 10 January 1928. Temporary accommodation was found in two pairs of newly built houses in Ida Road, which served until the premises were rebuilt and opened again in September 1931. In 1964 the Council moved to North Parade and the old building was demolished a year or two later.

North Shore golf clubhouse in 1920, now the North Shore Hotel.

North Shore Road, *c.* 1930, with the North Shore Golf Links on the left and the clubhouse in the background with a south extension added.

Scarbrough Avenue in the 1920s with, left to right, part of the Pier Hotel, Queens Terrace, the Kings Theatre and the indoor swimming baths. The hotel was gutted by fire in 1963 and the theatre and baths destroyed by bombs during the Second World War.

In 1929 the town bus service was shared by Skegness Motor Service and Tom Cary. This is one of Cary's (Vulcan) buses operating between North Shore and Seacroft – from one end of the town to the other – as the destination board indicates.

No. 63 Castleton Boulevard was erected soon after the dual-carriageway opened in 1934 and was a copy of the Sunway house in 'The Village of Tomorrow' at the Ideal Home Exhibition that year. Catalogued as 'representative of the most advanced ideas in design and construction', it cost £1,700. The Skegness replica was erected by developer George H. Hannam, who also built thirty contemporary semi-detached houses in nearby Castleton Crescent. No. 63 is now a nursing home.

A postcard view of the Young Women's Christian Association hostel in Drummond Road, postmarked 25 November 1921. The sender tells her friend in Birmingham that they are very quiet there, but are hoping to have visitors for Christmas. The hostel is believed to have closed around 1930 and the house is now part of the Leisure Hotel.

Winthorpe village school (top left) was built in 1865 and took up to fifty children of all age groups. It closed in 1951 when the Seathorne Junior School opened and the building is now incorporated in the Charnwood Tavern. St Mary's is Skegness's most beautiful church.

Skegness's first Baptist church, in Beresford Avenue, was erected in 1889 by St Paul's Free Church of England, a local group which had seceded from St Matthew's because of the rector's High-Church ritual. The breakaway congregation was forced to wind up five years later and the Baptists took over the corrugated iron building. When their present church opened in 1911 'the tin tabernacle' became the Sunday school.

In 1938 St Matthew's parish church
began to sink on its foundations and
expensive emergency repairs were
carried out, necessitating the closure of
not only the church, but also the
surrounding road and footpaths. The
photograph above shows the interior
strapped with timber while the work
was in progress. The foundation stone
had been laid in 1879 and the plan
showed a tower and spire (right), but
after the partly built tower started to
subside it was taken down and the west
end was completed with a light bell
turret. The 1930s problem, when the
whole building was sinking, was caused
by inadequate foundations and the
lowering of the water table through the
construction of impervious paths and
roads in the immediate neighbourhood
of the church.

St. Clement's Church, Skegness.

"Out in the fields, in solitude, alone,
  There stands a little church so old and grey;
A relic of the centuries that are gone,
  Forgotten by Time, defiant of decay.

No famous architect its form did plan,
  Its little nave and solid tower of stone;
It was erected in the times when man
  Built temples for the love of God alone.

Eight hundred years Destruction's ruthless hand,
  And Nature's war have left it standing there;
No useless ruin cumbering the land,
  But still the House of God, the place of prayer.

Brave little Church; Surrounded by the dead,
  Whose souls may visit us from realms sublime;
And sometimes joining when our prayers are said,
  May help to guard thee from the lust of Time.

That we may rest there when our work is done,
  Beneath thy shade, with feet towards the dawn;
Between the glorious sea and setting sun,
  Asleep until the Resurrection morn."

                                        A.M.F.

A postcard view of the old parish church of Skegness, with verses by an unknown poet written probably no later than the 1930s. The sixteenth-century church – making it rather younger than the 800 years reckoned by the poet – was erected after the great flood of 1526 swept away Old Skegness. The tower is believed to contain stonework salvaged from the church buried under the sea. When the resort town began building in the late 1870s, St Matthew's church, in the town centre, became the new parish church.

People and Events

The Skegness Jolly Fisherman, impersonated by Jimmy Loft in the 1920s. The long-serving comedian of Fred Clements' summertime shows was a great favourite, both on the sands at Happy Valley and at the Arcadia Theatre.

In the above photograph are some of the many committee and acting members of the Society during the 21 happy years. They are: Lady Montgomery-Massingberd, R. J. G. Dutton, Elizabeth Allan (vice-president), Gertrude Nelson, L. F. Hill, J. Huntridge, Cecil Hall, Constance Dutton, Edith Leslie, W. Wake, Evelyn Lill, Arnold Thorne, Raymond Heggs, Elsie Chapman, Edith Gale, C. H. Bray, Betty Lowndes, Cyril O. Shepherd and Mary Wheatley.

A collage reproduced from the *Skegness Standard* of 22 October 1958, on the occasion of Skegness Playgoers Society's twenty-first birthday. When formed in 1937 they gave fortnightly readings before going on to stage productions and an annual open play festival.

Skegness Playgoers Society in a reading of J.B. Priestley's *I have been here before* at the Baptist Hall in 1957. From left to right: Henry Wilkinson, Jean Hurt, Raymond Taylor, Edmund Sayer, William Bell, Winifred Wright.

A stage performance by Skegness Playgoers at Arcadia Theatre in 1951 of *Life with Father*, produced by Mrs Gertrude Nelson. The players are, back row, left to right: Molly Hird, Douglas Hill, Michael Procter, Phyllis Lill. Middle row: Vera Phillips, Peter Tingle. Front row: Alan Tish, William Nelson.

Skegness Amateur Operatic Society performing Gilbert and Sullivan's *The Pirates of Penzance* around 1930. Above, left to right: Reg Dutton, Harry Mather, Madge Walker, Herbert Burrell. The bobbies' chorus, below, was part of the same production.

The Curiosities Concert Party, produced by Mrs Cecil Hall, provided popular entertainment in the Skegness of the 1930s and she would bring the house down singing 'Jones of the Lancers' and 'You can't do that there 'ere!' Pictured at the Arcadia Theatre in 1936, from top and left to right: Gwen Bamber, Vera Phillips, Marjory Jackson, Kathleen Phillips, Elise Brown, Mary Greetham, Audrey Wallbank, Cecil Hall.

Skegness Choral Society began, in the late 1920s, as the Skegness Co-operative Choral Society and Miss Madge Walker was conductor almost the whole time until it disbanded in the early 1970s. This 1937 photograph shows, back row, left to right: -?-, -?-, Vincent Crane, -?-, Clifford Hannam, Douglas Hipkin, -?-, Herbert Walker, Bert Hillsdon. Second row: Alfred Denham, -?-, Miss Margaret Waite, Miss Mary Wheatley, Mrs W. Grunnill, Miss Wootton, Mrs Farmer, Mrs Walthall, Mrs Jones, -?-, Miss May Hincks, Jack Walker, ? Sharp. Third row: -?-, Miss Mary Hipkin, Miss Helena Walker, Mrs Keyworth, Mrs Brown, Mrs Waite, Miss Waite, Miss Sharp, Miss Madge Walker. Front row: Miss K. Simpson, Miss Marjorie Blanchard, -?-, Miss Day, Miss Betty Cooke, Mrs May Andrews, -?-.

Edwin Furniss and his Orchestra played in the Imperial Ballroom from the early 1930s until around 1950, as well as at numerous other dances and events in the town and district. Mr Furniss was a very talented musician and he was the musical director for the Operatic Society.

Jimmy Alldread and his Band, resident musicians at the Imperial Ballroom in the 1950s. Left to right: Ron Gosling, Cyril Arabin, Wilf Wilson, Jimmy Alldread (in dinner jacket), Russell Hill, Stan Cole, Sam Hayes (behind), George Goslow. Jimmy and his musicmakers also played over a wide area in East Lincolnshire, including Butlin's Holiday Camp.

The young man seen here with his sister was a boarder at Seacroft Preparatory School for Boys, Seacroft Esplanade, now a nursing home. He was to become Sir Frank Bowden, head of the Nottingham-based Raleigh Cycle Company. A few months before this 1919 photograph, the Dutch schooner *Europa* had crashed through the Pier and the gap it made is faintly visible.

Elizabeth Allan (1908–90), youngest child of Skegness GP, Dr Alexander Allan, became a film star in the 1930s, moving to Hollywood with Metro-Goldwyn-Mayer. Returning to England in 1937, she starred in the West End theatre and in Ealing films before making a new career in television, on the panel of *What's My Line?* and in other popular programmes. Educated at a Quaker school in Darlington, Elizabeth Allan married her manager, Bill O'Bryen. Her old home and father's surgery, Anstruther House, Drummond Road, was demolished in 1989 and the site is now a council car park.

George H.J. Dutton founded his business at Nos 43–5 Lumley Road in 1890, selling books, stationery and fancy goods, together with a lending library. Pictured in 1901, it was one of the largest shops in Skegness and closed in 1962 to become Lipton's supermarket. The building was demolished in the 1980s with new shops built on the site for Etam and Greenwoods.

Dutton's Stores celebrated its Golden Jubilee in 1940 under wartime conditions and this photograph of the family and staff gathering includes some Royal Navy guests from HMS *Royal Arthur*. Back row, left to right, between the naval men: Miss B. McTier, Miss J. McTier, Miss J. Overton. Second row: L. Potter, Mrs Potter, Miss Leary, Miss Jessop, M. Peet, Miss E. McTier, J. Veall, Miss G. Summers, K. Walls, Miss L. Hezzel, Miss B. Chapman, S. Dawson, Miss L. Twigg. Third row: Mrs D. Peet, Mrs G. Dutton, N. Walls, Mrs F. Walls, R.J.G. Dutton, Mrs G.H.J. Dutton, Miss G. Dutton, G. Dutton, Miss C. Dutton, D. Dutton. Front row: M. Dutton, Miss K. Walls, W. Buckingham, E. Walker, F. Dutton, V. Dutton.

The Sunday Morning Society in front of the Wesleyan Methodist Chapel, Algitha Road, 1905. Back row, left to right: G.H. Dales, Miss M.H. Phillips, Master H. Clark, Miss M. Smith, ? Hill, F. Searby, ? Midgelow, C. Girling, ? Rhodes, J. Wells, W.J. Garrard, J.T. Wholey, W. Taylor, W. Phillipson, W. Borman, ? Jeffreys, Master C.A. Green, Miss J. Smith. Second row: G. Goy, J. Fox, W.J. Smith, J. Wright, T. Bott, T. Cox, G.H.J. Dutton, J.W. Paddison, S. Chester, Mrs Chester. Front row: Mrs Fox, Mrs G.H. Dutton, J. Maxey, Mrs Bott, John Borman (leader), Mrs Cater, J. Simpson, Mrs Wells. The society held 9 o'clock prayer meetings before the Sunday morning service.

St Matthew's Church Gild of Servers, 1936. Back row, left to right: Don Cary, Clifford Hannam, Louis Walthall, Donald Wright, George Rowley, Edward Ball, John Campbell, Walter Chapman. Middle row: H. Daniels, Donald Slater, Raymond Ball, Jeffrey Kneen, Vic Burley, Jack Sanderson, Eric Welbourne, Jim Crawshaw, Howard Handley. Front row: ? Blewitt, Revd S.W. Bolden, Steve Rogers, Canon A.H. Morris (rector), B.C. Siddall, Revd W.R. Dewey, Norman Abbot. Chief server was Steve Rogers, while Louis Walthall was honorary secretary.

Hands in pockets, lads of the town take a Sunday afternoon stroll along Grand Parade in 1920. Only one is without hat or cap and all but two are in collar and tie.

Skegness National School class of 1927, snapped on the steps of the former Church Hall, Ida Road, just around the corner from the school, which was situated at Roman Bank. The 43 eleven- and twelve-year-old boys are, from left to right on the back row: John Burn, Ernest Burrows, Charlie Curtis, Ken Darlington, Peter Windley, Len Noseley, Ken Coultan, John Collier. Second row: Jeff Pearson, Frank Raynor, Sid Halliday, Archie Snell, Lew Boardman, Sid Bell, Alan Grunnill, Max Sleaford, Robert Goy, Gordon Allenby. Third row: Frank Saint, Joe Allenby, Rex Hunter, Herbert North, George Hufton, Frances Coulson, J. Green, J. Miller, Roland Wadds, Arthur Keyworth. Fourth row: Roland Jenkins, Alan Taylor, Jack Armstrong, ? Beecham, George Paddison, Jack Robinson, Harry Osbourne, John Parry. Front row: 'Bud' Stamper, Bert Sharman, ? Kerry, Ron Horwell, Percy Winfield, Dick Bell, Sid Ashton.

A group of visitors pose for their picture on the Pier, well prepared for the weather in 1920s fashions. The two similarly attired ladies in front could be sisters, while the older one, second from left, looks more like cartoonist Giles's grandma!

An all-male gathering near the Pier, in bowlers, boaters and flat caps, probably around 1910.

Celebrations in Lumley Square to mark the coronation of George V in 1910. On the right, schoolmaster Porter is conducting a choir; also on the right, the fire-alarm bell can be seen reaching above the rooftops. The railway station buildings form the background.

This ingenious turnout in an Edwardian carnival procession at Skegness has picture postcards stuck on the horse-drawn dray, with a smartly uniformed postman by the pillar-box. The inscription on the side reads 'Tinsel Post Cards'.

Skegness Police Superintendent Joseph Hutchinson and colleagues Sergeant Cross (left) and Constable Rodwell hit the headlines in June 1920 when they captured two armed men wanted for post office robbery and numerous burglaries. A nationwide search had been mounted for Topley and Ridley when, acting on 'information received', the three police officers cornered the robbers in their car at Thrall's Garage (now Safeway filling station). After a violent struggle, the robbers were disarmed and lodged in the cells at the former police station on Roman Bank. In recognition of their brave action, 'Long Joe' Hutchinson – he stood 6 ft 5 in – and his two assistants were awarded the King's Police Medal, presented by HM King George V at Buckingham Palace. The big policeman moved to Boston in 1924 as divisional superintendent and to Scunthorpe three years later where he finished his service in 1932. He died there in 1958, aged 75.

Skegness Aerodrome was established in 1931 in a field on Roman Bank at the north end of Royal Oak Terrace. The promoters were Capt. G.A. Pennington and Michael Scott and their sole flying machine was a Puss Moth three-seater monoplane. They ran a trans-Wash service to Hunstanton for £1 return, and short flights over Skegness for the holidaymakers, as well as occasional charter flights. A Skegness Aero Club was formed which organized the first air pageant in this part of the country, a display in 1932 attracting 15,000 spectators and including a race to Nottingham and back. This 1932 photograph shows the aerodrome's original Puss Moth and the petrol pumps on the right, which were used for both aeroplanes and road vehicles. The aerodrome closed in the Second World War and the site was later used for about thirty years as a YMCA holiday camp, shutting down in 1980. Meanwhile, the Aero Club had moved to a new site at Ingoldmells.

RAC Patrolman Sid Sellars travelled the main roads around Skegness in the 1920s, first on a bicycle and then on a motor bike and side-car. Besides carrying out roadside repairs for members, the patrolman was required to salute every driver that passed whose car displayed the club badge and, even in those days, there were enough motor cars to make it quite an arm-aching exercise.

T.A. Phillips' bread delivery van, photographed with William Winfield outside the Imperial Café in the 1930s. Phillips' confectionery shop was in Lumley Road, with the bakehouse at the rear in Prince George Street.

Skegness Army Cadet Corps in 1911 outside St Matthew's church, with the rector, Revd William Disney, centre. On the town war memorial, a few yards from where this photograph was taken, are the names of five Overtons, several of whom are in this group.

An Alfred Wrate photograph of what appears to be a First World War cavalry camp in the fields which at that time covered the space between Drummond Road and Briar Way. The Seacroft Hotel can be seen in the background, far right.

At the outbreak of war in 1939 a light anti-aircraft unit was formed in Skegness, shown (above) with Lt. R.S. Robertson, centre. The volunteers' headquarters was Hercock's former banana warehouse in High Street and as they drilled and marched in the town they suffered a lot of good natured banter as 'the Banana Brigade'. When part of 106 Light AA Battery, Royal Artillery, the banana boys saw active service in the Far East. Below, manning a Bofers gun at RAF Digby, near Sleaford, with Wilf Cussons on top and Harry Elvin, far left.

Skegness Home Guard in the Second World War. Back row, left to right: A.E. Sumner, J. Walker, J.S. Marshall, R. Francis, G. Wilkinson, C.H. Chapman, H. Botham, J.W. Ellis. Second row: J.L. Smith, H. Royce, C. Ranson, G. Perrin, J.G. Emson, J.F. Flint, S.W. Robinson, B. Mastin, A.W. Goy, W. North. Third row: L.H. Henshall, H. Chapman, C.H. Smith, H. Ainsworth, C.S. Blaze, G.W. Hazard, E.F. Hudson, E.C. Joslin, A.P. Smalley. Fourth row: E.V. Hydes, W. Smith, E.E. Andrew, W. Craven, D.W. Johnson, J.W. Moody, S.F. Hunter, L.N. Walthall, J.H. Postlethwaite, F. Innes. Seated: Lt. J.W. Poucher, Lt. R.M. Close, Lt. H.A. Gale, Capt. W.J.G. Kent, Maj. W.H. Major, Lt. R.W. Constable, Lt. K. Clarke, 2nd Lt. R.J. Scott.

The great freeze-up in the first winter of the Second World War cut off Skegness by road and rail for a week and naval recruits from HMS *Royal Arthur* (Butlin's Camp) helped to shovel away the snow. Skegness stationmaster, H.J. Osborn, is the central figure photographed on 30 January 1940 as the sailors cleared the railway line.

Skegness Land Army girl of the First World War, Elsie Wilkinson (afterwards Mrs George Eley), sowing winter wheat at Marsh Farm, Richmond Drive, in 1917.

Skegness lifeboat, *Anne, John and Mary*, photographed with crew and launchers, *c.* 1900. The lifeboat was in service from 1888 to 1906, with Thomas Smalley as coxswain until 1900, followed by John Smith Moody.

Lifeboat crew and launchers posed in front of *Cuttle*, 1954. Standing, left to right: Bert Hides, Don Bullen, Wilf Grunnill, Fred Miller, Phil Holvey, Jonny Strzelecki, Aubrey Patrick, Terry O'Reilly, Bill Perrin (coxswain), W.G. Bosworth. Seated: Len Cant, Herbert Sharp, Bert Holman, Bernard O'Reilly, Joel Grunnill, Lance Grunnill, Percy Grunnill. Willan G. Bosworth, Skegness Council's foreshore director was a guest at the practice launch which was about to take place.

Mercedes Gleitze became the first person to swim the Wash in June 1929, taking 13 hr 17 min. The Channel swimmer had arrived in Skegness a month earlier announcing her intention to make the crossing from there to Hunstanton, but after swimming 11 miles she had been forced to give up with cramp and cold. Miss Gleitze gave a swimming demonstration in Skegness bathing pool and then moved her headquarters to Freiston Shore and, after two unsuccessful attempts from Cut End, finally made the Norfolk coast from Butterwick. The distance in a straight line was about 16 miles although she would have swum a greater distance. She is pictured here after landing at Heacham, with Fred Munnings of Boston Swimming Club on the left. The Wash was finally swum from Skegness to Hunstanton on 26 May 1973 by 24-year-old Kevin Murphy, a Sutton-in-Ashfield journalist. Having already conquered the English Channel both ways and also the Irish Sea, he crossed the Wash in 13 hr 54 min.

Skegness Thursday FC, 1936–7, when they played in the Boston Thursday League. Back row, left to right: Trainer Walsham, Dick Raynor, Eric Gurnham, Sam Johnson. Middle row: George Brooks, Bill Key, Horace Dexter. Front row: Joe Kitchen, Cyril Price, 'Monty' Moncrief, Maurice Cash, Ron Horwell.

Skegness's two senior football teams never re-formed after the Second World War, but the new Skegness Town FC came into being in 1945 and became founder members of the Lincolnshire League in 1948. This was the 1947–8 team, with back row, left to right: Jack Vaughan (manager), Alf Smith, Ron Streets, Doug Cooper, Jimmy Plested, John Dowd, F. McKenzie. Front row: Gerry Parish, Albert Horsfield, Harry Hall, Roy Crane, Ken Northern.

Management personalities of Skegness Town Football Club, *c.* 1950. Left to right: Alec Sandaver, Norman Chase, Harold Swift, Walter ('Bib') Cook. The 1950s were the club's glory years when the Lilywhites were several times champions of the Lincolnshire League and the Central Alliance. In their first season in the Midland League they finished seventh to Peterborough United and an FA cup-tie with Boston United drew more than four thousand spectators to the Burgh Road ground.

Frank Bridle (standing), long-serving secretary of Skegness Wheelers and the Lincolnshire Road Riding Association, with the Revd F.W. Sykes, rector of Ashby-by-Partney, *c.* 1950. The latter was often to be seen along the country lanes on his trike, or with his wife on a tandem tricycle. In 1927 he covered 342 miles in a 24 hour time trial at Lincoln when nearing sixty. He died at Ashby in 1955, aged 86.

Skegness men's hockey team, 1929. Front row, left to right: W.A. Mountain, R.E. Frearson, E. Heaton (?), J.E. Searby (capt.), H.R. Searby, G.H. Black, -?-. The team were unbeaten in the five seasons from 1926 to 1931. John Searby played for Lincolnshire in 130 matches, 105 consecutively, and captained Skegness for thirty-three years. Henry Searby played more than a hundred games for the county and four times for England (from 1926 to 1931).

Skegness ladies' successful hockey team, photographed on the cricket ground c. 1930. Back row, left to right: Barbara Mountain, Helena Walker, Betty Burn, Dorothy Marshall, Dorothy Walker, ? Hudson. Front row: Margory Jackson, Kathleen Moore, Sadie Severn, Hope Hyams, Gladys Green, ? Frith, ? Hubbard.

Table tennis was a popular wintertime activity in Skegness from the 1930s right through until the 1950s. The popular venues were the Imperial Café and the Red House Hotel, and the Tigers, Linnets and other teams competed in a local league, with inter-town matches drawing large audiences. Grosvenor Tigers' team in the 1930s are, left to right: Dick Dunkley, Edmund Sayer, George Walker, Jim Spence.

A table tennis prize presentation at the Imperial Café, *c.* 1950. Left to right: Colin Chapman, John Spence, George Hart, Joan Toon, Rita Winn, Sid Fennell, Joan Bellamy, Rex Musson, Ron Wiggett, Reg Sayer.

The Skegness to Horncastle walking race setting out from Lumley Square on 27 June 1923, with thirty-seven competitors. The 21½ mile marathon was essentially a Horncastle event – entrants had to be residents of the town – and it was being revived after a lapse of twenty years. The row of cottages in the background was later demolished to make way for the gas showrooms and public lavatories. The race is still a popular annual event.

The pace-setters striding uphill through Burgh. No. 21 in the leading three, on the right, is Sid Stone, the event winner in 3 hr 50 min.

SECTION FOUR

Around and About

Hanson's Mill, *c.* 1900, on the hilltop at Burgh-le-Marsh. It was built in 1852 on the site of an earlier post-mill and worked until the 1930s. The sails were removed in 1938 and after standing derelict for half a century it was converted to residential use in 1990.

The church of St Nicholas, Addlethorpe, *c.* 1920. It is noted for its medieval wood carving and is outstanding in an area of fine churches.

Addlethorpe and Ingoldmells carrier, Josiah Simpson, photographed with his family and carrier cart at Addlethorpe, *c.* 1900. He took passengers and goods to and from Spilsby and Alford markets, every Monday and Tuesday, in the days when there were no cars or buses.

West Street, Alford – quite traffic-free in 1904. The thatched buildings are one of the town's most charming features. Just past the disused Wesleyan Chapel (1864), behind the trees, is the thatched Manor House, now a folk museum.

South Street, Alford, and the Primitive Methodist Chapel of 1856, long closed for worship. The adjoining houses have disappeared altogether.

The Windmill inn and market place, Alford, near the beginning of the twentieth century (above), and in the 1930s (below). The inn saw the inauguration, in 1780, of the Stuff Ball, a great society event to encourage Lincolnshire industry. The ladies were required to wear gowns made of 'stuff', wool produced and woven in the county. The magistrates court was conducted at the Windmill and the Customs and Excise was also located there, the officer in 1764 being Tom Paine, afterwards a champion of American independence and author of *The Rights of Man*.

Alford market place in 1905, with Barclays Bank (left) and most of the other buildings still in place today. The iron posts also remain, but the chains and cobblestones have gone and the area is marked off for car parking, but filled with stalls on market days.

South Market Place, Alford, was the old market place, photographed by Mrs Nainby in 1908, with Barclays Bank on the right. The pedimented building on the left is the Mechanics' Institute of 1854, a Victorian contribution to adult education, with a library and lecture room for evening classes.

Alford Toll Bar at the foot of Miles Cross Hill, photographed by Edwin Nainby in the 1890s. The Alford and Boston Turnpike began operating in 1786, and the first toll bar was nearer the town, by the Tothby Lane junction. Tolls were lifted in 1878.

A market-day scene in Alford in 1910, with prospective buyers testing some of the articles before the auctioneer starts work.

Stones' Cycle Works and ironmongery premises in South Market Place, Alford, 1908, with agricultural implements displayed on the forecourt. Joseph Stones at this time was advertising Rover and Triumph bicycles and was a repairer approved by the Cyclists' Touring Club. The buildings were later demolished to make way for the central car park.

At the same date, 1908, A.W. Holmes's South Bridge Motor and Cycle Depot in Alford competed for customers with a roadside showroom displaying both forms of travel. Mr Holmes also sold petrol, no doubt in tin cans, as petrol pumps and filling stations were at that time in the not-too-distant future.

H. Walker & Co.'s drapery and millinery stores at Nos 1, 2 and 3 Cheapside, across the road from the churchyard. It was one of Alford's largest shops, established by J. & J. Bryant. In 1908 they were advertising in a local guidebook as linen and fancy drapers, milliners and dressmakers, tailors and breeches makers. Part of the premises has long been occupied by the Co-op.

Walker's shop caught fire in March 1911 and, although the premises were badly damaged, much of the stock was salvaged and put on sale in the Corn Exchange at knock-down prices. This was the hats and caps stall, attracting a lot of attention in an age when headgear was almost as important as footwear. Mr Lill of Hogsthorpe, mac in hand, fitted himself up with a topper for the benefit of the photographer.

The Coronation Day procession, for the crowning of King George VI in 1937, moving along East End in Alford, past the former cattle market.

The coronation gathering in South Market Place, with Stones' Cycle Works in the background.

East End, Alford, photographed by Mrs Nainby in 1908. The row of thatched cottages on the left is long demolished. The white building in the far distance is Walker's drapery shop.

Chauntry Road, Alford, viewed from near Parsons Lane, with the Congregational church (1877) and other buildings still almost as they were when Edwin Nainby took this picture in the 1890s. Scissor-grinder John Minkley appears to be chatting with a customer on his door-to-door round.

Station Road, Alford, 1910. Queen Elizabeth's Grammar School (right) was founded in 1576 after William Cecil, first Lord Burghley, petitioned the queen to grant a charter for a free grammar school in Alford. The boys' school moved to the building seen above in 1881, since when it has been enlarged several times and became coeducational in 1959.

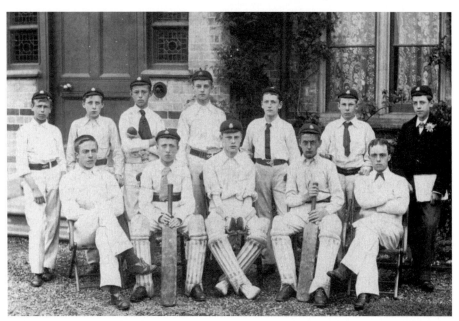

Alford Grammar School's cricket XI, 1899. Standing left to right: F. Barnes, E. Thompson, H. Gibbons, H. Spofforth, J. Richards, J.R. Bryant, H.W. Seymour. Seated: Mr W. Horn, L. Coney, L. Wood (capt.), W. Morrell, Mr A. Kewley.

Anderby Creek in 1952, with houses and bungalows on top of the grass-covered dunes. In the foreground is the drainage tunnel where Anderby Main Drain, collecting surface water from the surrounding fields, discharges into the sea.

A few months later, the great flood of 31 January 1953 left the white, flat-roofed house and its neighbours at Anderby Creek balanced precariously on the edge of a sandy precipice.

Burgh-le-Marsh, 1903. Perhaps a better name would be Burgh-on-the-Hill as it rises on a slope where the marsh meets the Wolds. The majestic church of St Peter and St Paul dominates the scene, with the smoking chimney of Wharram's brewery adding an industrial touch.

Burgh once had two parish churches, but St Mary's was destroyed in the sixteenth century. This postcard view must have been an artist's impression of what the building might have looked like, with a tiered tower, a thatched roof and a disproportionately long nave.

Burgh-le-Marsh High Street, *c.* 1912. The National School (right) was erected in 1840 at the expense of the vicar, Revd Sir George Crauford who built the hall about the same time. The school closed in 1986 and, thanks to the efforts of the local community, it became the present recreation centre. The tall building with three chimney-pots is the Bell Hotel.

George W. Mackinder opened his Burgh Post Office Stores in Church Street in 1900, selling groceries and drapery. Pike's guidebook, ten years later, mentioned that he had just added a lending library and departments for stationery, glass and china, toys and fancy goods. This picture postcard was posted in 1915.

Billy the Drover (left) and Rocky White were familiar figures in Burgh-le-Marsh in the early twentieth century, as they herded sheep and cattle to Spilsby and other markets in the area. The two old toppers lived together in Burgh, their real names being William Ambrose Smalley and Isaac Wright. Rocky was once knocked down by a ram in a field near Spilsby and suffered a broken leg. The animal stood over him for several hours and he feigned death until at last it wandered off and he was able to drag himself to the road to await help. Rocky died early in 1939, shortly after Billy. They are seen here in Spilsby, probably in the 1920s.

Waite's coach and carriage works in Burgh's West End in a posed study near the beginning of the twentieth century. The two-storey timber building, looking so spick and span in this picture, still stands but has been in a state of near collapse for a number of years.

Harry Abbott set up as a threshing contractor in Burgh-le-Marsh in the late 1870s, first with portable engines drawn by horses and then with Lincoln-built Foster traction-engines. At the turn of the century, Abbott & Sons had six threshing sets and the Station Road firm closed in 1942. The top picture shows Abbotts working with a Foster engine, *c.* 1920, and below, an earlier scene using a portable engine with a tall smokestack and a very large flywheel.

St Paul's Missionary College in Burgh-le-Marsh, shown in, probably, the 1930s, was dedicated on St Paul's Day 1878, having been previously in use as a school for ten years. During its near sixty years' existence the theological college trained young men to go out as missionaries of the Church of England to all parts of the world. At the closing-down service in 1936 the sermon was preached by the Bishop of Zululand, a former student. The building reverted to school use and was demolished in 1968, the site now taken up by a housing estate.

The Mission Church, as it was usually called, was actually a chapel of ease for isolated parishioners of Burgh-le-Marsh. It was built in 1867 as the gift of William George Tozer, vicar of Burgh-with-Winthorpe, who became successively Bishop of Central Africa, Jamaica and Honduras. Dedicated to All Angels, the chapel could accommodate sixty people, and services were frequently conducted by students from St Paul's Missionary College in Burgh. Disused for many years, the building was shortly to become a flag factory when my photograph was taken in 1982.

Candlesby High Street in the 1920s when it carried the main road traffic. The A158, with a much wider carriageway, still winds through the village, but now misses this narrow street where the front doors come almost up to the road. The tall chimney belonged to Eagle's bakehouse.

Stan Parkinson in 1924 with the horse and cart with which he delivered bread from his uncle Horace Eagle's bakery in Candlesby, covering many miles a week on his country round. Mr Parkinson delivered bread for over forty years, afterwards with Edwards & Chapman of Skegness and then for Mother's Pride.

Candlesby Hill, pictured from the west in 1906. On the hilltop, Candlesby House stands on the left and Hill House on the right, but the lone cottage on the hillside has been replaced by modern houses. The stream, a tributary of the River Lymn, still flows under the road – the wooden handrails are now metal – but the footpath signpost and stile are no longer there.

A Primitive Methodist circuit gathering of local preachers in Chapel St Leonards, c. 1920. The one lady appears to be quite at ease among the sixteen gentlemen.

John Henry Canning opened the Café Marina, near the pullover in Chapel St Leonards, around 1920 and it became a popular eating-house and dance hall for both visitors and residents. Pictured in the early 1930s, the building was burnt to the ground in 1941.

Chapel Point with a woven tree branch barrier, in the early twentieth century. Willoughby High Drain has its outfall here, discharging surface water from the surrounding farmland.

The seashore near Holland's Gap, Chapel St Leonards, in the 1920s. Grass-covered dunes, part natural, part man-made, provided the main bulwark against the sea until reinforced concrete began to take over in the twentieth century. The great flood of 1953 finished off most of the remaining sandhills, depriving the visitor and the coast-dweller of what was a lovely part of the landscape, but it was a forced sacrifice in the interests of public safety.

Bathing machines, bell tents and wooden huts have all served as changing rooms on the beach. On even more occasions, in the interests of modesty, bathers have made do with mackintoshes or just a towel, performing amazing contortions to complete the difficult task of taking off and putting on. These neat little canvas cubicles at Chapel in the 1930s allowed the changing exercise to be completed in comparative comfort.

Four coastguards occupied the white-walled cottages at Chapel St Leonards in the latter part of the nineteenth century. Photographed in 1925, the cottage block stands in the lee of the sand dunes, with ready access to the seashore.

The last of Chapel's three lifeboats, *John Alexander Berrey*, in service from 1888 until the station closed in 1898. Coxswain Matthew Grunnill, afterwards coxswain at Skegness, is standing far left. The lifeboat station had opened in 1870 and the boathouse, with an added storey, is now Mr Hoyes' stores.

Chapel St Leonards suffered great damage in the disastrous storm surge of 31 January 1953 and, as the concrete defences crumbled, many dwellings like these were surrounded by the North Sea.

New sea defences in hand following the 1953 flood. The old village had been washed away in 1571 and the later disaster destroyed houses, farm buildings, crops and caravans, leaving the village open to still further inundation.

Croft wheelwright and blacksmith shop, *c.* 1930, was operated by the Sanderson family from before the First World War. As tractors replaced horses, the trade turned to machinery repairs and, in 1965, Roy Sanderson, grandson of the founder, began designing and manufacturing forklifts. The business expanded rapidly, employing several hundred workers until recession cut markets and forced the company to close in 1990.

Croft Grange (photographed by Raymond Taylor in 1979) was the family home of Katherine Heanley, one time sweetheart of Francis Kilvert, whose *Diary* is now a literary classic. Kilvert called her his 'sweet Katherine Mavourneen', but the romance petered out. Katherine never married and she was matron of Boston Hospital when she died suddenly at the age of 41 in 1891. Kilvert's cousin, Adelaide Cholmeley, had married Charles Heanley in 1874 and they went to live at Clough Farm, not far from Croft Grange. Katherine was cousin to them both and was a bridesmaid at the wedding where she first met the Revd Francis Kilvert.

When the Wainfleet to Skegness rail extension opened in 1873, the intervening stations were called Croftbank and Cowbank, but were afterwards renamed Havenhouse and Seacroft respectively. A light railway ran from Worth's Farm alongside the road and over the river carrying produce to goods wagons at Havenhouse station. Nearer Skegness, it was not unknown for train travellers destined for the Seacroft district of the resort to alight at Seacroft station and find themselves marooned amid the turnip fields, far from sea and town. Seacroft station closed in 1953. Both the photographs were taken by Raymond Taylor in 1979.

Firsby railway station in the 1880s. It was part of the East Lincolnshire Railway, running between Boston and Grimsby which was completed in 1848. When branches were opened to Spilsby (1868), Wainfleet (1871) and Skegness (1873) the small, isolated village took on new life. The three trains, left to right, are bound for Spilsby, Boston and Skegness. The bottom photograph was taken shortly before the station closed in 1970. Wainfleet and Skegness trains left from the open platform on the far right.

The Railway Hotel, near the level-crossings at Firsby, *c*. 1970. The hotel opened soon after the new railway came into being in 1848, and when the line closed in 1970 the hotel's days were numbered also.

Firsby windmill, *c*. 1910, when the miller was John Appleby. The windmill stood close to the boundary with Irby, but Mill Lane is the only reminder of its existence. It was demolished in 1923.

The Barley Mow (pronounced locally to rhyme with 'cow') stands at a crossroads on the A52 at Friskney, *c*. 1910. The board on the gable-end shows John T. Simpson as the landlord and he may be the gentleman standing near the first door, while the postman is about to clear the wall letter-box, which still survives today.

Fold Hill, *c*. 1930, with Kitching's Mill which began working in 1824. The windmill and the white cottage have long gone, the latter replaced by modern bungalows, but the large house which was once Panton's general stores is still standing. Fold Hill's elevation above the surrounding land can now be measured in centimetres, but it was probably once a slight eminence of dry land amid the watery fens.

The mill at Friskney Tofts in running order in the 1920s, worked by the last miller, John Chapman Stephenson. The pointed roof building on the right was the bone-crushing mill for making artificial fertilizer. The former post-mill at Friskney Tofts stood back from the A52, a short distance north of the Barley Mow. The date 1720 was cut in the centre post and another carved inscription read: 'Joseph Wakelin kept this mill in the years of Our Lord, 1733–54.'

The mill in 1934, now with only two sails remaining. After further storm damage it was dismantled five years later. The mill had to be turned to face the wind by the long tailpole seen projecting over the steps.

Friskney Feast, on the second Monday in June, is a great day for the village, dating back more than a hundred years. The Sunday school children were carried round in decorated drays, travelling into Wainfleet where the feast was held in the Methodist schoolroom. This was one of the turnouts in 1904.

A decorated dray posed in Wainfleet market place in 1914, the last occasion the Friskney feasters travelled there. Bill Simpson stands by his horse's head. The June event is still held but, because of heavy traffic on the main road, the parade is confined to the village.

Teacher and pupils at Friskney Eaudykes School, 1934. Left to right, back row: Miss Hubbard, James Fletcher, Kenneth Farr, Leslie Hewis, Gerald Simpson, Edward Toynton. Middle row: Doreen Turner, Joan Clow, Dennis Baker, James Cooper, Cecil Grant, Fred Toyne, Edith Tidd. Front row: Bessie Grant, Dorothy Grant, Jack Chapman, Francis Sands, Gerald Simpson, Frank Simpson, Vera Martin. The Eaudykes School closed in December 1947.

Schoolmaster Robert Robinson stops for a chat with Mrs Johnson at Vicarage Cottage, c. 1903. He was master of Friskney National School for forty-three years from 1880 and in retirement was parish clerk and active in numerous local organizations. The cottage, between the vicarage and the church, looks rather different today without its thatched roof.

Cockling by the water's edge at Friskney Flats in 1890. George Dinnis Bray (1835–1912) earned a living, like his forebears, gathering cockles and trapping wildfowl in nets stretched along the seashore.

The Friskney village postman was a man to look up to at the beginning of the twentieth century when he went round on his high bicycle. Here he is dropping a letter at Tommy Bray's house in Sea Lane.

Gibraltar Point warden, Wilf Holland, with several rabbits hanging from his bicycle's handlebars in the 1920s. The dunes at Gib are still honeycombed with rabbit burrows, screened by the silver-green buckthorn bushes. The gravel barges, *Gleaner* and *May Queen*, can be seen anchored in the river.

Wilf Holland's children, Joan and John, photographed beside the Haven, Gibraltar Point, in the 1920s.

Tennyson Farm, or Sykes's Farm, stood back from the west side of the road, half a mile from Gibraltar Point, but all except a few outbuildings have gone. Tommy Greetham (left) was tenant from before the First World War until the early 1920s.

Gibraltar House, once the Ship Inn, has long
disappeared and only a single sycamore tree –
on the left approaching the main car park –
remains to show where it stood. The house
was the home of the Perrins and then the
Hollands in the 1920s, when the few visitors
to Gibraltar Point were often glad of a bottle
of pop from Mrs Holland's refreshment stall.

In the early part of this century, two ex-Thames barges carried cargoes of sea gravel from Heacham and Snettisham across the Wash to Skegness. The owners were two Skegness businessmen, Jim Giles and George Hyams, but when they dissolved the partnership in the early 1920s the two boats were left to rot in a creek off the Haven at Gibraltar Point. They were eventually burnt, but this is one of them in the 1950s.

Gunby Hall, *c*. 1910. The hall was erected by Sir William Massingberd in 1700, when some of the building material was brought by sea from Hull and landed at Skegness and Wainfleet. Traditionally, Gunby, in its lovely park, is the house Tennyson had in mind in *The Palace of Art* as 'a haunt of ancient peace'. Field Marshal Sir Archibald Montgomery Massingberd and his wife, Lady Diana, occupied the Hall when it was handed to the National Trust in 1944.

Halton Holegate and the 'hollow gate', or cutting, through the green sandstone, near Spilsby, *c.* 1930. The rectory is on the left and the church on the opposite bank, while the former footbridge over the road provided the incumbent with a short cut to work.

Halton Holegate and the Bell Inn in the 1930s. Fixed to the wall, on the far right, can be seen one of the Automobile Associations's round, yellow and black metal name-plates displaying the village's name, a useful device seen at the entrance to most villages at that period. The white, thatched cottage is no longer there and Halton hides just around the corner, hardly seen from the main road.

Harrington Hall, pictured in the early 1900s, is associated with Tennyson's poem, *Maud*, based on the poet's own disappointed romance with a young lady who once lived there. In the latter half of the twentieth century it was the home of local MP, Commander Sir John Maitland and had been sold only a year when it was almost destroyed by fire on 4 November 1991; it is now fully restored.

Hobhole Drain, near Midville, in the 1930s. The drain provided one of the main water channels when the East Fen was drained, carrying the flood water fourteen straight miles, from the edge of the Wolds to empty into Boston Haven. The East Fen, south and west of Wainfleet and Friskney, was once an area of swampy land and small 'deeps', or ponds, and was one of the last parts of Fenland to be drained, early in the nineteenth century.

Hogsthorpe South End, with William Neal's hardware shop at the end of High Street, in 1921. Kelly's Directory for 1922 shows that, in addition to Neal's shop, Hogsthorpe had 3 grocers, 2 butchers, a baker, confectioner, bootmaker, men's hairdresser, cycle agent, joiner, bricklayer, plumber, 2 blacksmiths, a wheelwright and a coalmerchant. George Young kept the post office and Robert Falkinder the Saracen's Head. There were also 22 farmers, 4 smallholders and a poultrykeeper. The 1921 population was 511.

Hogsthorpe's Thames Street, *c.* 1922. Road traffic does not appear to be a problem and Kelly's county directory at that date mentions that 'a motor bus passes from Chapel every Tuesday for Alford at 9.30 a.m., returning same day at 3 p.m.'.

Hogsthorpe High Street, 1906. The street today looks very much like it did then, except that children no longer play on the road. A butcher is still there, but not Walter Wright. The low, white building has gone – Tom Stones' blacksmith shop – but St Mary's church tower can still be seen peeping over the rooftops.

Hogsthorpe High Street, c. 1910, with the Saracen's Head, then kept by Mrs Sophia Muntus. The lantern-lit entrance to the churchyard is on the extreme right and, on the road, a single pony and trap poses little danger to the children eager to get in the picture.

Hogsthorpe, like other Marshland villages strung along the A52, stands on a hummock of boulder clay rising above the surrounding silt. At the 1851 religious census, St Mary's church congregation averaged 100 in the morning and 150 in the afternoon. South Street Wesleyans' two Sunday services aggregated 540, while the Bethel Primitive Methodist chapel held three Sunday services with 250 worshippers altogether. Hogsthorpe's population at that date was just under a thousand. The church is photographed around 1900.

Huttoft Mills in 1905, when Fred Lowe was the miller. Huttoft windmill worked for more than a century before gale damage forced its closure in 1945 and it was then gutted and used as a grain silo.

Huttoft and a carefully posed picture of its Post Office Stores in 1910. Mr Cash stands in the doorway with his assistants nicely spaced and Dobbin dutifully quiet in the shafts of the delivery van. Cash's Stores is now a private residence.

A view of the north side of Huttoft in 1920, when the A52 was more like a country lane. The thatched mud and stud cottage on the corner of Jolly Common Road was pulled down several decades ago, but the signpost pointing to Jolly Common is still there.

Huttoft School group in front of St Margaret's church, 1922. The village school –
happily still in use, near the church – bears a stone inscribed: 'Huttoft School, 1840.
Prov. XXII, 6', referring to the Bible proverb, 'Train up a child in the way he should go,
and when he is old he will not depart from it.'

The Wesleyan chapel, Huttoft, beside the main road (A52) which was not very wide in
1910. Huttoft Methodist church, still neat and trim, is a plain brick building, typical of
numerous other village chapels of the mid-nineteenth century. The view across the fields
to the parish church is now obstructed by other buildings.

The Mastin family had not long taken up residence at The Haven, Ingoldmells, when the sea broke through, *c*. 1920. The house was situated at what is now the northern end of Funcoast World and George Mastin and his wife are seen here standing extreme right and left in the flood water, with the sandhills just visible in the background. Thirteen-year-old Kathleen Mastin and young Tom are on the garden seat, with Gilbert afloat in the bathtub and Victor standing just behind. Connie Mastin is partly hidden between two other ladies at the back. The Haven stood on the sea side of Roman Bank where the Ingoldmells road turns inland, but at that time it was a 'T' junction before the present slip road was made and it came to be known as Mastin's Corner. Below, The Haven shows its scars after the 1953 flood and it was afterwards demolished with the site incorporated in Butlin's Holiday Camp.

The White House on the sea bank at Ingoldmells was farmed by the Hallgarths from about 1880 and at the beginning of the present century Mrs Hallgarth began to take visitors into the eight-bedroomed house, with more in tents in the field. Right from the beginning there was flooding at spring tides with the constant task of bolstering up the sea bank. By 1911 most of the defences were washed away and the farmhouse was vacated as the Hallgarths emigrated to Australia. Photographed soon after that date, the building slowly crumbled away to finally disappear in the great storm surge of October 1922.

A collapsed caravan camp at Ingoldmells in the much greater flood of 1953.

Café and caravan camp at Vickers Point, Ingoldmells, 1950. In the 1953 flood the fragile structures were wrecked and tossed away as the waves tore through the defences, engulfing the fields over a wide area. Below, note the round, metal 'pork pie' ex-army huts from the First World War, and the tiny 'sentry-box' lavatories near the wire fence. The Bell Inn now stands on the site of the former café.

Two work gangs employed building Butlin's Holiday Camp at Ingoldmells in 1935. The top picture was taken during the construction of the sewage disposal plant. The work was carried out by direct labour and was far from finished the following Easter when 500 campers were accommodated in very spartan conditions.

The Railway Queen of Great Britain, Irene Eaton, at Butlin's Holiday Camp, Ingoldmells, in 1937, pictured with her Maids of Honour and Skegness stationmaster, H.J. Osborn. The famous Butlin chef, Joe Velich, was well in the picture, as usual.

HRH the Duke of Edinburgh with Billy Butlin on his right, visiting the holiday camp on 23 September 1949 to receive a large cheque for the National Playing Fields Association. Cllr R.J.C. Dutton, chairman of Skegness District Council, is walking just ahead of the policeman. They are photographed in front of Butlin's Ingoldmells Hotel.

A collage of some of the guest stars appearing in Butlin's Skegness Holiday Camp at Ingoldmells in the 1930s. Clockwise from top left: Lew Stone and his Band, boxing champion Len Harvey sparring with the fighting kangaroo, Scots comedian Will Fyffe, Mantovani and his Tipica Orchestra, Gracie Fields, Jack Doyle – the singing Irish heavyweight boxer, Elsie and Doris Waters, music hall favourite Florence Desmond.

The Roundhouse with octagonal walls at Langton-by-Spilsby was built as a lodge to Langton Hall. Bennet Langton entertained his great friend, Dr Samuel Johnson, at the hall in 1764 and the famous man of letters would no doubt have taken note of the unusual thatched building. The pillar-box on the right and the pantiled privy are no longer there, but the Roundhouse remains and is still occupied.

The ford over the Langton stream has long been covered over, but when my photograph was taken in 1938 cyclists and other road users splashed through the shallow water. The raised footpath is now overgrown, but the ornamental gate remains, although with only one of its unusual two-way hinges. The red brick church dates from 1725 and was highly praised by Poet Laureate Sir John Betjeman.

Markby thatched church – 'the only one in England' according to the caption on the postcard – was built from the fragments of a moated priory established about 1160. The tiny church stands just off the A1111, midway between Alford and Sutton and has been neatly rethatched since this 1930s photograph was taken.

Markby church interior, again in the 1930s, with box pews and the dog-tooth chancel arch, the latter from the former priory. An oak chest is also believed to have been made from the beams of the monastic building. The date 1611 is inscribed on one of the tie beams of the present church.

Monksthorpe Baptist chapel, in the middle of nowhere, was erected in 1701 when Nonconformists, in spite of new Toleration Acts, were still being persecuted. It was built by the Baptists of Burgh, well off the beaten track, disguised as a barn among the trees. The high hatch in the wall was for the preacher to escape through, should he be warned of an approaching mob. This photograph of the shored-up church was taken by Henry Wilkinson in 1982, with the author (left) and the late Archer Osbourne. The chapel stands on the north perimeter of the wartime Steeping Aerodrome.

The open baptistry, beside Monksthorpe Baptist chapel, where total immersion was practised. Both chapel and baptistry have been allowed to deteriorate sadly and the stables where the worshippers left their horses is in an even worse state. A restoration scheme is now being discussed and the chapel was rededicated in 1992. This photograph was also taken in 1982.

Mumby and the Red Lion in the early 1920s. Across the road, George Cowburn, blacksmith and motor engineer, had his workshop and a small 'Union Jack' BP sign on a post indicates that he also supplied petrol. The white, thatched cottage and the rectory behind the trees have long since disappeared.

Mumby School group, photographed by Edwin Nainby of Alford, in the 1890s. It includes all age groups, from beginners to school-leavers.

Mumby post-mill at the beginning of the twentieth century. The mill, long gone, was built in 1688 and stood on the high ground behind the village post office. A great storm hit the Lincolnshire coast in 1880, when the shore was littered with wrecked ships and, as the gale threatened to blow down the mill, villagers held on to the sails and substructure until the wind had died away.

Partney in the 1920s, with a motor car standing outside the Victory Hall, erected to commemorate the First World War and located between the churchyard entrance and the village stores. The hall was replaced by a brick building in 1986.

The White Horse Inn, a Soulby pub, stood on the site of the present Victory Hall in Partney, next to the church entrance, before the First World War.

Partney water-mill, powered by the little River Lymn, was located near the foot of Blue Hill on the road to Spilsby. From the eighteenth century until 1929, when it ceased working, it was kept by the Goodwin family. Cornelius Goodwin, miller and cornmerchant, was said to set the price of corn at Spilsby Corn Exchange and when he died he was reckoned to be one of the wealthiest men in the region. A weir is all that remains to mark the place of the old water-mill, pictured here around 1900.

Partney's church of St Nicholas whose tall greenstone tower at the junction of the A158 and A16 is seen by thousands of motorists on the way to the coast every summer. The decayed oak tree in the churchyard is said to be more than a thousand years old and two or three centuries ago, when in its prime, the branches hung across the road. The tree is still there and this is how the church looked at the beginning of the present century. The end of the former White Horse Inn can just be seen on the right.

Partney post office in 1924, when George Bailey was the sub-postmaster. A lady cyclist and a Model T Ford appear to be on the point of departure. Partney's post office is no longer there and has changed its location several times in the present century.

School Hill on the A16 at Partney, leading to the churchside junction with the A158, at the beginning of the century. The cottages still stand on the raised pathway behind the railings, and the former school, converted to smart housing, is away from the road on the left.

Raithby Hall was the home of Robert Carr Brackenbury and when John Wesley came to visit his old friend in 1779 he found he had made a chapel over one of the stable buildings (above). Wesley preached there on four occasions and on his last visit, in 1788, he called Raithby 'an earthly paradise' where he would gladly have tarried had he not been 'a wanderer upon earth', destined to find rest only in another world. The key to the chapel can be obtained on enquiry at the hall, which is now a nursing home. The photograph below was taken probably in the 1920s and the one above in the 1980s, but the hall has changed little in a hundred years.

Scremby and the thatched cottage standing below the green knoll topped by the tower of Grebby Mill, *c.* 1905. It was one of several similar labourers' cottages belonging to the seventeenth-century Scremby Hall, one of the grandest country houses in the neighbourhood. For many years the hall was the home of the Brackenburys, but it fell into disrepair in the 1930s and the last part was taken down forty years later. The neatly thatched cottage now has a matching extension.

In the Lincolnshire edition of *The King's England* (1949), Arthur Mee described Skendleby as 'one of Lincolnshire's most charming villages'. It still is, and its single street with raised pavement stands undisturbed and peaceful a mile and a half from the main road traffic hurrying towards the coast. It is pictured here in the 1930s.

Sir John Franklin's bronze statue in Spilsby, 1925. The statue, unveiled in 1861, commemorates the Spilsby-born explorer who discovered the North-West Passage connecting the Atlantic and Pacific Oceans in the Arctic. His two ships became trapped in the ice and Sir John with his 134 men perished in 1847. The Terrace is a raised and railed pavement in front of the shops on the right.

Spilsby High Street on a picture postcard posted in 1914. W.K. Morton's printing and stationery shop had been the birthplace of Sir John Franklin in 1786 and it is now a bakery.

Spilsby Sessions House, with its massive Doric portico, was completed in 1826. The Quarter Sessions for South Lindsey were held here and a House of Correction, or gaol, at the rear of the premises was used until 1876. The Sessions House closed in January 1981, the magistrates court moving to Skegness and the building was later converted to its present use as a theatre. The picture shows the building as it is today, unaltered since the last century.

The Avenue, 1907, was once the drive leading to Eresby Hall, former seat of the Willoughbys whose monuments are a feature of Spilsby parish church. Burnt down in 1769, all that remains of the hall is a tall gate pier. The pretty tree-lined pathway is now a tarmac road called Eresby Avenue.

Spilsby British Legion on a Remembrance Day parade soon after the end of the Second World War. In the lead, carrying a cane, is the grammar school headmaster, A.W. Nesbitt.

James Badley in the doorway of his Spilsby High Street ironmongery shop in 1905 with one of the bicycles he had just brought in as a new line. The cycle business quickly developed and soon Mr Badley was moving onto motor cars, becoming one of the leading motor agents and repairers in the area. Percy Cople is standing on the right.

SPILSBY FOOTBALL TEAM

WINNERS OF THE

Lincolnshire Association Challenge Cup

AT

BRIGG

8th APRIL, 1882

Spilsby Football Club was a founder member of the Lincolnshire Football Association in 1881 and, although a minnow among larger towns like Grimsby, Boston and Grantham, they soon showed they could more than hold their own. When the new body established the Lincolnshire Challenge Cup competition (forerunner of the Lincs. Senior Cup), Spilsby won the trophy three years running. The hat trick was completed with a 4–2 victory over Grimsby Town in 1884 and when the triumphant team reached home they were paraded round the town with a torchlight procession preceded by the town band. Spilsby's 1882 winning team, from top, left to right, shows: J. Southby; C. Miller, H.R. Bellamy; J. Searby, R. Driffield; W. Shaw, J.H. Barratt (capt.), H. Robinson; B. Robinson, H. Allington, H. S. Mawer.

Spilsby Board of Guardians outside the Gables Hospital (the former union or workhouse), Hundleby, 1929. The Spilsby Union was established in 1838 under the Poor Law Act (1834) and the governing board was formed by representatives of nearly seventy parishes. On the front row, left to right: -?-, A. Allewell (New Leake), -?-, -?-, E.P. Rawnsley (Raithby), Capt. W. Hoff (Scremby), Mrs Grantham (Skegness), Maj. Maddison (Steeping), -?-, T. Gwilym Jones (clerk to the Guardians), -?-, -?-, -?-, H. Hoyles (Alford), W.J. Stone (Old Bolingbroke). Other Skegness members are Samuel Moody, extreme right on back row, and John Borman, fifth from left on middle row.

Spilsby Rural District Council at Toynton Hall in 1966, with Chairman Cllr T.N. Cade (Brinkhill) in front wearing his chain of office, Vice-chairman Cllr F. Read (Ulceby) on his left and Clerk of the Council T.H.E. Cottell on his right. The occasion marked Mr Cottell's retirement after almost forty years with the RDC, most of the time as clerk.

Spilsby Volunteer Fire Brigade with their hand pump appliance outside the long-vanished Old Hall in High Street, 1896. The 'civilian' driver, Joe Atkin, was employed at the White Hart as ostler and coachman, conveying patrons and their luggage to and from the railway station in the hotel's private carriage.

An open-air baby show at Spilsby in 1917 draws quite a crowd, with men in khaki mingling with the mothers and prams.

Spilsby railway station, *c.* 1912. The branch line from Firsby Junction had opened on 1 May 1868, financed by a local company, but operated by the Great Northern Railway who also provided rolling stock. There was only one intermediate station, at Halton Holegate. The GNR took over the complete installation in 1891, at a cost of £20,000. Passenger services were withdrawn in 1939 and the last goods train left Spilsby station on 30 November 1958. The bottom picture shows the engine with crew and station staff on that occasion.

Steeping Aerodrome, officially RAF Spilsby, operated with Lancaster bombers of 207 Squadron, seen above. The station was operational from 1943 to 1945 and was designated a reserve airfield for the USAAF during the Korean War of the 1950s. A memorial in Great Steeping church commemorates the 511 airmen of 207 Squadron who sacrificed their lives and another 109 who were made prisoners of war. There is a separate memorial in the church for 44 (Rhodesian) Squadron RAF.

Steeping Aerodrome from the air. The road from Gunby can be seen on the right, forking right towards the airfield near the former Rising Sun. After it was restored to agriculture some of the airfield roads were taken into the public highway system and one of the hangars has survived. The former railway line between Firsby and Burgh can be seen across the bottom right hand corner.

Toynton Hall at Toynton All Saints, in the 1950s. The hall was situated 2½ miles south of Spilsby, and was the headquarters of the former Spilsby Rural District Council, one of the largest RDCs in Lincolnshire. The hall was built in 1908 on the site of an earlier house.

Wainfleet Haven, or Steeping River, with the pointed roof of the pinfold among the trees on the left. It was used by the pinder to pen straying cattle and sheep and a fee had to be paid before the animals were released. The photograph was taken probably in the 1950s.

Wainfleet market place, *c.* 1930, with a Progressive bus stopped on its journey between Skegness and Boston. The red brick Clock Tower was officially opened three months before Skegness Clock Tower on 2 May 1899. It commemorates Walter Martin of Wainfleet Hall and was erected by his widow and presented to the town. She married a second time, rather unhappily, and as Mrs Martin Simpson became a prominent Skegness resident, dying in 1951, aged 96.

Several women are sitting on the steps of the Buttercross, on the right, in this 1910 photograph of Wainfleet market place. It was from the Buttercross that John Wesley preached a sermon on Sunday 18 June 1780, the day after his seventy-seventh birthday.

The Magdalen College School (pronounced Maudlen) was founded in 1484 by William of Waynflete, the town's most famous son who became Bishop of Winchester, Lord Chancellor and founder of Magdalen College, Oxford. It provided secondary education for the locality during four and a half centuries, until replaced by Skegness Grammar School in 1933. In 1951 it became the Magdalen Secondary Modern School until that moved to a new building and it is now the Wainfleet branch of the County Library. The school is pictured here in the 1920s.

Wainfleet Magdalen College School's soccer team, 1926–7. Back row, left to right: Dick Bellamy, C.S. White, Arthur Barton, Ted Grunnill, Wilf Parsons. Middle row: Claude Allen, John Farrar, Gilbert Allen, Len Allen. Front: S. Swaby, Reg Newbitt.

Wainfleet Salvation Army Corps near the turn of the century. The corps was formed in 1884, its citadel being a former poultry auction building in St John Street. It was next door to the Wesleyan Methodist chapel – a rival business, one might say – but the two denominations seemed to coexist quite amicably, although, when the later arrivals formed a band, the Wesleyans probably muttered among themselves about their noisy neighbours.

C.N. Parker's grocery and drapery at No. 4 High Street, Wainfleet, near the beginning of the century. In more recent times this fine looking three-storey building has been Saddler's Foodstore.

The tall town houses filling both sides of Wainfleet's Barkham Street have always looked strangely out of place. They were built in 1847 by the London Bethlem Hospital on land bequeathed to them by Sir Edward Barkham and the same architect had designed similar terraces for them in the totally different surroundings of Southwark. This 1904 photograph shows Holmes's butcher shop at No. 2, on the right, and Camp's clothing store across the road, which was demolished to make way for the Coronation Hall which opened in 1913.

Northolme Hall, Wainfleet, probably in the 1920s, with what appears to be a bull-judging event in progress. Wainfleet Northolme, or Wainfleet St Thomas, was once a separate parish with a church last mentioned in the seventeenth century. The churchyard is now Northolme Cemetery whose entrance archway is the town war memorial.

Wainfleet Bank and the churchyard – a mile beyond Crow's Bridge – where the parish church of All Hallows stood, then at the heart of medieval Wainfleet, with ships sailing into the busy little port. After the building collapsed it was replaced in 1821 by the present parish church of All Saints. The railed tomb is that of the father of William of Waynflete who built the school. Close by, a plain slab covers the grave of Sir Edward Barkham, lord mayor of London, who died in 1669. Both tombs stood inside the walls of the former church. The photograph was taken in the 1980s, although the scene has remained unchanged for many years.

Wainfleet Dramatic Society playing *Dear Octopus* in 1949 with, left to right: Joy Disney, Joan Howsham, M. Dobson, Pat Banham, Janice Sutton (front), Pat Reeves and Elmer McClure. The young Janice Sutton was even then showing talent that was to bring her fame in the world of theatre and dance.

Wainfleet Women's Institute in the early 1950s at the former Quaker meeting house in High Street, where they held their gatherings. Front row, left to right: Susan Hewison, Mrs Blanchard, Mrs Reeves (president), Mrs Jones (secretary). Also in the picture are Mmes Hildred, Collins, Quickfall, Hewison, Johnson, Stubbs, Cash, Simpson-Eyre and Misses Waite and Blanchard.

Well Vale, near Alford, is a jewel on the edge of the Wolds, with the early eighteenth-century hall (now a private school) overlooking a tree-bordered lake. In his *Highways and Byways in Lincolnshire* (1914), W.F. Rawnsley called it 'the prettiest spot in the county'. The postcard view (top) is from a Nainby photograph and, below, the Lincolnshire Pageant is performing in the grounds in 1933.

Welton-le-Marsh Post Office Stores, kept by Thomas Bush in 1912. The PO Stores is now on the main road and the earlier establishment is a private house on the corner of Beck Lane.

Willoughby, pictured here in the early 1900s, was the birthplace, in 1580, of the redoubtable Captain John Smith, soldier, explorer and adventurer, but perhaps best remembered for his connection with the Indian princess, Pocahontas. He was baptized in the parish church, where he is commemorated by a fine stained glass window and other memorials, one of which says that John Smith was 'first among many leaders of the settlement of Jamestown, Virginia, in 1607, which began the expansion overseas of the English speaking people, of the Commonwealth of Virginia and the United States of America'.

Willoughby railway station, *c.* 1960. The tall chimney beyond the railway bridge belonged to Clover Dairy, an important milk distribution centre, established in 1934. Company lorries collected churns of milk from the farms and, after pasteurizing, it was sent off to the retailers, some by train as far as London. As doorstep delivery changed to sealed bottles, Clover Dairy installed a bottling plant in 1953. The dairy closed down in 1978 and the chimney, so long a local landmark, was finally demolished.

Willoughby's flower-bedecked railway station was the junction for the Sutton-on-Sea line (1885), later extending to Mablethorpe and forming a loop to Louth. The Sutton branch went off to the right at the end of the platform. Willoughby station closed in 1970.

Acknowledgements

The author is grateful for the loan of photographs from the following, used in addition to the illustrations from his own collection:

Alford Queen Elizabeth Grammar School • G.H.F. Atkins • Mrs N. Badley
Mrs Nan Bresley • Butlin's Holidays • Hedley Cook • T.H.E. Cottell
George Cowham • Mrs E. Elvin • Ken Epton • George Farr
Mrs Dorothy Farrar • Mick French • Colin Handley • Miss Fran Hanson
Henley RAF Museum • John Hewitt • Mrs Helena Hipkin • Paul Linder
Jeff Morris • Miss José Osborn • Stanley Parkinson • Dennis Plant
RAF News • Bob Riddington • Fred Sellars • *Skegness Standard* • John Spence
Richard Stainton • Jonny Strzelecki • Raymond Taylor • Mrs Vera Taylor
Henry Wilkinson • Percy Winfield • Ronald F. Wright